Honesty

BY CYNTHIA AMOROSO

Published by The Child's World®
1980 Lookout Drive • Mankato, MN 56003-1705
800-599-READ • www.childsworld.com

Acknowledgments
The Child's World®: Mary Berendes, Publishing Director
The Design Lab: Design
Christine Florie: Editing

Photographs: iStockphoto.com/CEFutcher: cover, 1;
all other images © David M. Budd Photography

ISBN 9781623235208
LCCN 2013931449

Printed in the United States of America
Mankato, MN
July, 2013
PA02172

ABOUT THE AUTHOR

Cynthia Amoroso is Director of Curriculum and Instruction for a school district in Minnesota. She enjoys reading, writing, gardening, traveling, and spending time with friends and family.

Table of Contents

What Is Honesty?   4

Honesty at School   6

Money Mistakes   8

Honesty and Cheating   10

Honesty and Waiting   12

Taking the Cake   14

Honesty at Home   16

Honesty and the Lost-and-Found   18

Honesty Is Important!   20

Glossary   22

Learn More   23

Index   24

What Is Honesty?

Have you ever told a lie? Have you ever tried to cheat? Everyone has times when they could lie or cheat. But honesty means telling the truth. It means not cheating. Honesty is not always easy. It takes strength. But it is the right thing to do. And it feels good!

Honesty feels better than cheating!

Honesty at School

Your teacher gives you homework. She tells you to do it over the weekend. You end up playing with friends. You forget all about your homework! On Monday, your teacher asks for the homework. You show honesty by telling the truth. You do not make **excuses**. You do not **copy** another student's work.

Sometimes telling the truth can be scary.

Money Mistakes

Maybe you like to go to the store after school. Your **favorite** gum costs 50 cents. You give the clerk one dollar. She should give you 50 cents back. But she gives you 75 cents by mistake. You know she gave you too much money. You show honesty by telling her she made a mistake. You give the extra money back.

Honesty means not taking more than your share.

Honesty and Cheating

You are playing a board game. You are unhappy because your friend is winning. He goes to the kitchen for a snack. You could move your piece farther ahead. Then you might win! But you show honesty by not cheating. You follow the rules—even if it means you will lose. Maybe you will win next time!

Honesty and Waiting

The swirly slide is the best thing on the playground. Kids are lined up, waiting to use it. You are waiting your turn. The person in front of you looks the other way. There is room in front of her. She might not notice if you went ahead. You show honesty by waiting your turn.

Honesty means being fair about taking your turn.

Taking the Cake

Your dad has baked chocolate cake. He made it to take to a party. Chocolate cake is your favorite! It looks really good, and you are hungry. You eat a piece. Your mom sees that some is missing. She wants to know who ate it. You could blame your younger brother. But you show honesty by telling the truth.

Honesty means telling the truth—even if it will get you in trouble.

Honesty at Home

Your older brother has some money. He leaves it on the table. It would be easy to take it. You could put it in your piggy bank. He would not know where the money went. But you show honesty by leaving the money alone. You tell your brother where he left it.

Honesty means not taking things that belong to others.

Honesty and the Lost-and-Found

You and your friends are playing at the park. You see a bag near the swings. There are toys in the bag! Somebody has forgotten to take them home. You would love to have some of the toys. But you know they belong to someone else. You show honesty by taking them to the lost-and-found.

Honesty means returning things that are not yours.

Honesty Is Important!

Honesty shows people that you tell the truth. It shows others that they can trust you. People want friends who are honest. They want family members who are honest, too. People will trust you when they know you tell the truth!

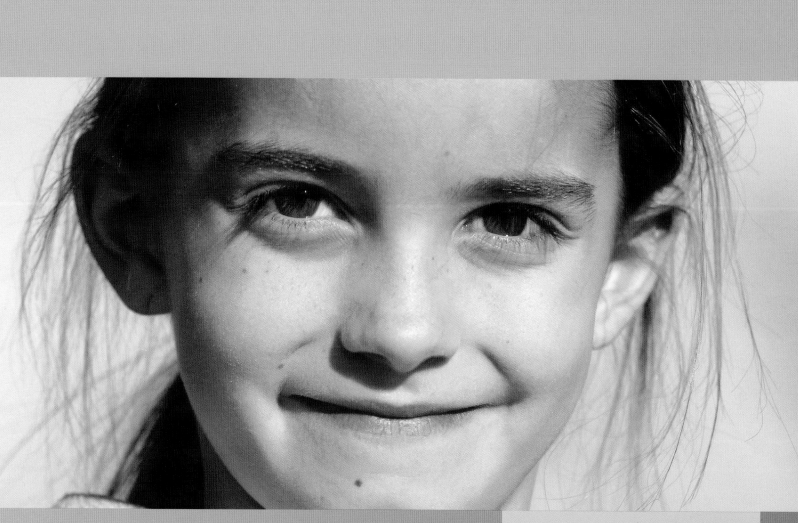

It is nice to be trusted!

Glossary

copy—When you copy something, you do it exactly as it is done somewhere else.

excuses—Excuses are reasons why you did not do something.

favorite—When you like something best, it is your favorite.

Learn More

Books

Binkow, Howard. *Howard B. Wigglebottom and the Monkey on His Back: A Tale about Telling the Truth.* Marina Del Rey, CA: Thunderbolt Publishing, 2010.

Levins, Sandra. *Eli's Lie-O-Meter: A Story about Telling the Truth.* Washington, DC : Magination Press, 2010.

McGuire, Andy. *Eleanor the Hippo Learns to Tell the Truth.* Eugene, OR: Harvest House Publishers, 2011.

Web Sites

Visit our Web site for links about honesty: childsworld.com/links

Note to Parents, Teachers, and Librarians: We routinely verify our Web links to make sure they are safe and active sites. So encourage your readers to check them out!

Index

Belongings, 18
blaming, 14

Cheating, 4, 10
copying, 6

Excuses, 6

Family, 14, 16, 20

Lying, 4, 14

Money, 8, 16

Park, 18
playground, 12

School, 6

Teacher, 6
trust, 20
truth, 4, 6, 14, 20

Waiting, 12